Montem Primary School
Hornsey Road
London N7 7QT
Tel: 020 7272 6556
Fax: 020 7272 1838

Montem Primary Scho
Hornsey Road
London N7 7QT
Tel: 0171 272 6556
Fax: 0171 272 1838

The Shakespeare Collection

RICHARD III

RETOLD BY JAMES RIORDAN

Illustrated by Stephen Player

an imprint of Hodder Children's Books

 *Character list:*

Richard, Duke of Gloucester
(later, King Richard III)

King Edward IV
(Richard's brother)

George, Duke of Clarence
(brother of Edward and Richard)

Queen Elizabeth
(Edward's wife)

Duke of Buckingham
(Richard's ally)

The young princes

Edward, Prince of Wales   **Richard, Duke of York**
(Edward's elder son)   (Edward's younger son)

Lady Anne
(later, Richard's wife)

Henry, Earl of Richmond
(later, King Henry VII)

Duchess of York
(mother of King Edward, George and Richard)

Lord Hastings
(the Lord Chamberlain)

Lord Mayor of London

Sir James Tyrrel
(who kills the princes)

Background to our story

Many centuries ago, England was at war with itself. It was the time of the Wars of the Roses, named after the red rose emblem of the noble Lancaster family, and the white rose emblem of the noble York family.

York eventually won and, in 1461, the Duke of York became Edward IV of England. The Lancaster survivors fled to France. They included young Henry, Earl of Richmond.

Towards the end of his reign, in 1483, the dying King Edward prepared to pass the crown to his young son Edward, Prince of Wales. But Richard, Duke of Gloucester, the King's younger brother, had other ideas ...

Richard, Duke of Gloucester, had a mind as crafty as his body was twisted. Women turned away in disgust from him, and dogs barked at his crooked shadow. But the more he was hated, the more wickedly Richard behaved.

"I'll outwit them all," he vowed. "A glorious summer of peace has followed the dark winter of war, and now the king is only interested in dancing and feasting! But who wants that? Not me! *I* plan to be King!"

Richard had hatched a cunning plot. First he would get rid of his brother George, Duke of Clarence. He knew that the shock of Clarence's death might kill their elder brother, the king. Edward was ill, after all ...

The plot was beginning to work. Thanks to Richard, the king's mind had been filled with prophecies of betrayal. One night, he dreamed he was about to be stabbed by somebody whose name began with 'G'.

"My brother George, Duke of Clarence!" the king had cried. And although he loved his brother, he had been too frightened to ignore the warning.

"Lock him in the Tower," he ordered. "He must be executed!"

Richard's next plan was to woo Lady Anne, whose father, Henry VI of Lancaster, and husband he had killed in battle. At her father's funeral, she accused him of murdering them, but he blamed the deaths on his mad love for her.

"Your heavenly face drove me to it," said Richard.

But Anne spat fiercely in his face, crying, "I wish my spit were poison, you foul toad!"

"Poison could not come from so sweet a mouth," replied Richard, kneeling. "Take my sword and kill me for my crimes."

He was so flattering and persuasive that finally Lady Anne took the ring he offered her.

When she had gone, Richard chuckled, "Was ever a woman so easily won? It is only three months since I killed her husband! Still, I won't keep her for long, that's for sure."

With George, Duke of Clarence, in the Tower, Richard knew he had to move fast. The king might have a change of heart at any moment and release him. Richard hired two murderers to kill his brother.

After tricking their way past the guards, the murderers stabbed Clarence and hid his body in a barrel of wine. "That'll finish him off!" they laughed.

At the palace, the sick king had gathered his rival nobles together to swear friendship with one another. It was a happy, peaceful scene, with which Richard joined in at once.

"There's not an Englishman alive I'm not friends with!" he lied.

Then Queen Elizabeth asked her husband to pardon the Duke of Clarence. "It's already done. I've sent an order to set Clarence free," replied the king happily.

"But ... I'm afraid the gentle duke has been executed," announced Richard. "Your pardon arrived too late."

The shocked king rounded on his nobles, crying, "Why didn't any of you beg for his life? God forgive me!"

Within a few days, the king was dead. In all the grieving that followed, no one shed more tears than Richard. But behind his mask of sorrow, he was plotting more evil.

Richard decided that the queen's brothers, Lord Rivers and Lord Grey, could be a threat, so he had them imprisoned. He also spread rumours about the queen, saying that Clarence's death had been her idea. Now, only the young princes, Edward, Prince of Wales, and Richard, Duke of York, stood between Richard and his ambitions. He had to get them out of the way. But how? He hatched a plot as cunning as it was wicked ...

As Lord Protector, who better to 'protect' the young princes than their kind uncle? So it was Richard and Lord Buckingham, his friend and ally, who escorted the young Prince of Wales to London for his coronation.

Then, pretending to be concerned for their safety, Uncle Richard told his nephews, "You'd better stay in the Tower's royal rooms until the coronation."

But the princes were unhappy with this idea.
"So wise, so young, they say, never do live long,"
chuckled Richard at this.

"I shan't sleep peacefully there," said the young
Duke of York. "I'm afraid of my Uncle Clarence's
angry ghost. My grandmother says he was
murdered there."

"Well, *I'm* not afraid of dead uncles," said the Prince of Wales.

"Nor of living uncles, I hope," said Richard with a wicked smile, as he and Buckingham led the princes to the Tower.

No one apart from Buckingham knew about Richard's evil ambitions, but people were beginning to grow suspicious. They began to take sides – and anyone who opposed Richard ended up losing their head.

Richard wondered if Lord Hastings, King Edward's former chamberlain, would support him as king. He sent a messenger to find out secretly, and also to invite Hastings to a meeting about the coronation at the Tower. When he heard that Hastings' loyalties were to Edward's family, Richard decided he must die.

During the meeting, Richard talked of plans to kill him by witchcraft. "Oh yes, look at my body, all bent and twisted. It's the doing of that witch Queen Elizabeth and her devil sons. What do you say to that Hastings?"

"*If* it is true my lord ..." gasped Hastings.

"Don't talk to me of 'ifs', you traitor!" said Richard. And he ordered his guards to take him away, crying, "Off with his head! I want it on a plate before me!"

$\mathcal{A}$ few hours later, Richard and Buckingham met the Lord Mayor of London before the Tower walls. Just then, a servant arrived, carrying Hastings' head on a silver dish. "Here is the head of the traitor, my noble lord," he said.

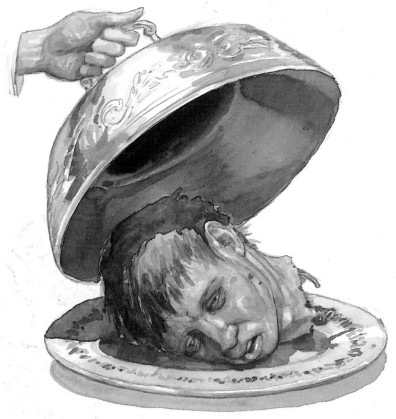

To the mayor, Richard said sadly, "I so loved the man. Yet he was plotting to murder me!" The tears flowed freely down his cheeks.

"I'm sure he deserved to die for his treason," said the mayor, taken in by Richard. "I will go and tell the people so."

So far, all was going to plan. But if he was going to succeed, Richard knew he needed the support of the people. He told Buckingham to go to the Guildhall, with messages for the mayor and the citizens.

"Tell them the princes are the brats of a servant girl with no claim to the throne. Mention that their father, Edward, was also a bastard. Say that *I* am the rightful king! Tell them that no one is braver in battle, wiser in peace, more kind or modest ..."

Just to make sure the people would be convinced, Richard sent a dozen of his own men to the Guildhall. They stood at the back of the crowd, ready to throw up their hats and shout: "God Save King Richard, England's Rightful King!"

But the plan failed. Although Richard's men shouted out three times, the people stood as silent as statues. Richard would have to try something else. "Bring the Mayor and the citizens to Bayard Castle," he told Buckingham.

When Buckingham arrived at Bayard Castle with the Mayor and a crowd of citizens, Richard's servant told them, "The Lord Protector is praying and can see no one."

But eventually Richard appeared, standing between two bishops and holding a prayer book.

He listened quietly, with his head bowed, while Buckingham told the crowd that he was the true successor to King Edward.

"It is your right of birth, blood to blood," Buckingham said, turning to Richard. "Your loving friends want you as king."

"Your citizens beg you," added the Lord Mayor.

But Richard pretended to have none of it.
"No, no, no. Your love deserves my thanks. But I must refuse. I have so many faults. And the royal tree has left us royal fruit: Prince Edward. I will not accept!"

But the crowd would not listen. Richard had no choice but to give in.

"Long live King Richard!" cried Buckingham and everybody cheered.

Richard was to be crowned king the next day.

On the day of Richard's coronation, Elizabeth went to visit her sons in the Tower. Their grandmother, the Duchess of York, and Lady Anne, who was now Richard's wife, went too. But the chief guard barred the way. "The king's orders are to let no one in," he said.

"The king! Who is that?" they asked in astonishment. When they heard it was the Lord Protector, Richard, Elizabeth said angrily, "The Lord protect him if he thinks *he's* king!"

The news struck everyone present like a death blow. Then one of Richard's allies came to take Lady Anne to Westminster to be crowned.

"I hope I die before I hear the words 'God Save the Queen!'" whispered Anne in despair. Indeed, it would not be long before her life was ended.

Even though Richard was now King, he was still restless. "I want the two princes dead," he told Lord Buckingham.

But this was going too far, even for Buckingham. "Give me time to think it over, My Noble Lord," he said.

Richard realised that he had lost Buckingham's support, but he didn't care. He soon found a man who would agree to do his dirty work: Sir Richard Tyrrel. When Tyrrel returned from the Tower, Richard was waiting eagerly. Did he bring news that would make him a happy man?

"Yes, Your Highness. You can be happy," said Tyrrel.

"Did you see them dead?" asked Richard.

"I did, my Lord," replied Tyrrel.

Richard rubbed his hands with glee. "I've killed my brother Clarence, my two nephews are dead – and Anne, my wife, has said goodbye to this world!" he said to himself. "So, next I must marry my niece, Princess Elizabeth, Edward's daughter. Richmond has his eye on her. I must move quickly!"

When news of the princes' murder reached
Queen Elizabeth, she went with the Duchess of
York to the palace, to confront Richard. The
Duchess told her son that she wished she had
strangled him in her womb. Then she cursed
him: "Bloody you are, bloody will be your end;
your life is full of shame, and shame will be your
end in battle!"

Elizabeth added, "Amen to that." But Richard
only said, "Stay, madam, I want a word with you
about your daughter, Princess Elizabeth."

Afraid for her daughter's life, Elizabeth began pleading with Richard. "But I want her to be my queen," he said. "Persuade her to agree, and your future grandsons will one day be kings!"

Seeing this as a better fate than death, Elizabeth agreed. "Take her my true love's kiss," said Richard, smiling.

But Richard was not to enjoy his bloody triumph for much longer. A messenger had arrived with troubling news.

"Henry, Earl of Richmond, is sailing to England from France. He comes to claim the crown."

"How many men has he?" asked Richard.

"Six or seven thousand," said the man.

Richard sneered. "We have three times that number."

"There is more," added the man. "Some of your noble lords have thrown in their lot with Henry, and the Duke of Buckingham is raising an army against you."

Richard waved a hand impatiently. "No one can defeat me. My name itself is a tower of strength. Summon my army!"

Then more news came – Buckingham had been captured by Richard's allies. "So much for Buckingham!" said the king and ordered his execution. Then, at the head of his army, he set out to meet Richmond. The battle was to take place at Bosworth Field, near Leicester.

The king's army was large in number, but weak in spirit. Richard's supporters were tied to him by fear. No one trusted him – and he trusted no one in return.

For the first time, Richard's conscience began to trouble him. The night before the battle, he

settled down to sleep in his tent. But the ghosts of all his victims appeared in his dreams – and promised that he would meet death tomorrow.

The hovering ghosts of the two princes cried out, "We shall haunt you in the battle. Think of how you killed us – and die!"

The ghost of Clarence cried in a hollow voice, "Tomorrow, think of me. I, too, will haunt you. Despair and die!"

The ghost of Lord Buckingham wailed, "I was first to help you win the crown and last to feel your tyranny! Die tomorrow in guilt and terror!"

More ghosts appeared: King Henry VI, his son Edward, Lady Anne, Lord Hastings. Richard woke up in terror, putting his hands up to fend off the ghosts. They faded away and he was alone again.

"Why does my conscience torment me?" he moaned. "No one loves me. Even if I die, no one will pity me!" Then he grew angry. "It was only a dream! I'm not scared of *anyone*."

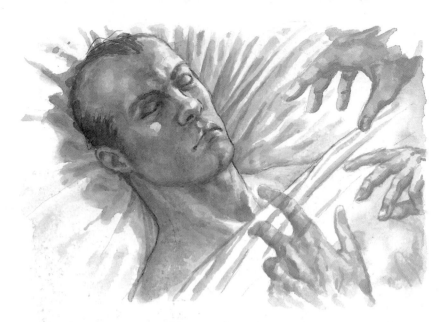

On the other side of the battlefield, Henry, Earl of Richmond, was sleeping soundly in his tent. He too was visited by the same ghosts. Their message, however, was quite different.

The ghost of the young princes cried, "Sleep well, Henry. Sleep in peace and wake in joy. Live long and become a good king."

The ghost of Clarence told him, "We all pray for your victory. May God keep you safe." And the ghost of Hastings spoke up, "Win the day – for England's sake."

*N*o sun greeted the dawn, and the dew was raw and cold. It promised to be a black day for someone. But for whom? Richard or Henry?

Richard's servants strapped on his armour and prepared his white charger. Then he rode forward to greet his army, wearing the crown of England. His men waited on the battlefield: horsemen with lances, archers with bows, foot soldiers with swords.

"Sound the drums and trumpets!" cried Richard and rode boldly forward at the head of his great army.

From out of the rolling mists, Henry and his men rode towards him. The thunder of horses' hooves mingled with the shouts of the men, and the sound of arrows flying through the air.

Many of Richard's men turned and fled, but not Richard. Charging forward on his horse, he fought with the strength of ten. And when his horse fell beneath him, he sprang up, crying out for another, "A horse! A horse! My kingdom for a horse!"

Richard and Henry came together, swords at the ready. With a heavy blow, Henry killed his rival and, holding up Richard's severed head, cried out, "Victory is ours. The bloody dog is dead!"

When the fallen crown was placed on Henry's head a great roar rolled across the battlefield, greeting England's new king.

King Henry VII soon brought together the families of York and Lancaster by marrying Princess Elizabeth. At long last, the white rose was united with the red, and England entered a period of true peace.

The Shakespeare Collection

Look out for these other titles in The Shakespeare Collection:

Julius Caesar Retold by Kathy Elgin
Julius Caesar is the leader of Rome, but the power has gone to his head. Even his best friend Brutus can see that this tyrant has to be stopped for the good of the people. But when Brutus finds himself involved in a plot with Cassius to kill Caesar, he wonders if any good can come from the murder ...

King Lear Retold by Anthony Masters
King Lear has set his daughters a test to prove how much they love him. Goneril and Regan flatter the old king, but his youngest daughter, Cordelia, loves him too much to play the game. In a moment of anger, Lear banishes Cordelia. Can any good come out of this rash decision?

As You Like It Retold by Jan Dean
In the magical forest of Arden, it seems, people can catch love like the flu... Celia loves Oliver, Rosalind loves Orlando, and Phebe loves Ganymede. Everything should be perfect. But Ganymede is really Rosalind in disguise, and Orlando has no idea. Will anyone live happily ever after?

You can buy all these books from your local bookseller, or order them direct from the publisher. For more information about The Shakespeare Collection, write to:
The Sales Department, Hodder Children's Books, a division of Hodder Headline Limited, 338 Euston Road, London NW1 3BH.